BY THE
PEOPLE

E PLURIBUS UNUM

THE U.S. SUPREME COURT

Bill McAuliffe

Creative Education ★ Creative Paperbacks

TABLE OF CONTENTS

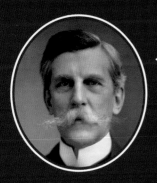

William Marbury thought he had the job locked up.

THE U.S. SUPREME COURT

President John Adams, during his last days in office in 1801, had filed the papers to make Marbury a justice of the peace. But the new president, Thomas Jefferson, didn't want Adams's appointees around. He purposely delayed the papers. Before the Supreme Court, Marbury argued that he'd been hired for the job. The court agreed but said there was a little more to it. The court found that the law setting up the selection process was unconstitutional. It tried to give the court powers beyond those granted by the United States Constitution. Therefore, the court didn't have the power to help Marbury. However, it claimed a more profound power for itself—the ability to judge whether laws passed by the people are legal, "to say what the law is." That landmark opinion made the Supreme Court an equal among the three branches of the U.S. government.

The Supreme Court met at the U.S. Capitol from 1801 to 1935.

JUDICIAL BRANCH

Court system

THE PRESIDENT NOMINATES FEDERAL JUDGES AND SUPREME COURT JUSTICES.

THE SUPREME COURT CAN DECLARE PRESIDENTIAL ACTS UNCONSTITUTIONAL.

CONGRESS HOLDS THE POWER OF IMPEACHMENT.

THE SUPREME COURT CAN DECLARE CONGRESSIONAL LEGISLATION UNCONSTITUTIONAL.

CONGRESS HOLDS THE POWER OF NOMINATIONS AND APPROVES PRESIDENTIAL

E PLURIBUS UNUM

BY THE PEOPLE

EXECUTIVE BRANCH

President

THE PRESIDENT CAN VETO CONGRESSIONAL LEGISLATION.

CONGRESS MAY IMPEACH FEDERAL OFFICERS AND OVERRIDE PRESIDENTIAL VETOES.

LEGISLATIVE BRANCH

Congress

The system of checks and balances ensures that no one person or group holds too much power.

CHAPTER 1

A SLOW START

THE U.S. SUPREME COURT

As the Revolutionary War ended, the states were governed by the Articles of Confederation. The national government under the Articles was weak, with no ability to collect taxes. The Articles also didn't establish a central court system. Disputes between states were difficult to resolve.

Representatives drafted the Constitution in 1787 to address some of those problems. The first three articles established the branches of government: the executive, led by the president; the legislative, meaning Congress; and the judicial, which is the court system. Each branch has powers to limit the actions of the others. This system of checks and balances is one of the key methods by which the nation's founders tried to prevent any single arm of government from having too much control.

NYC EXCHANGE BUILDING, 1790

★ The court held its first session in New York City in 1790. But it ... didn't deliver its first opinion for 18 more months. ★

A SLOW START

The Constitution set up the court system in a mere six paragraphs of the four-page handwritten document. Article III establishes "one Supreme Court." It also allows for "inferior" courts as Congress finds necessary. The Supreme Court's jobs are to resolve conflicts that arise in the workings of the Constitution and U.S. laws; to settle disputes involving treaties, ambassadors, and **maritime** affairs; and, in particular, to straighten out arguments between the states and their residents. That sounds like a simple and short to-do list. But in the past 200-plus years, the Supreme Court has addressed controversies and crises the authors of the Constitution never envisioned.

The very first bill introduced in the U.S.

Senate was the Judiciary Act of 1789. It established a Supreme Court of six judges, or justices. It also set up 13 judicial districts. Supreme Court justices were required to hear cases twice a year in each district. The court held its first session in New York City in 1790. But it spent its first meetings on organizational issues and didn't deliver its first opinion for 18 more months. As a result, in those days, the Supreme Court was hardly noticed.

The circuit court duties presented another problem. Not many people were eager to take a job that required traveling long distances twice a year by horse or stage-coach over dangerous roads. Even people accomplished in the law and dedicated to

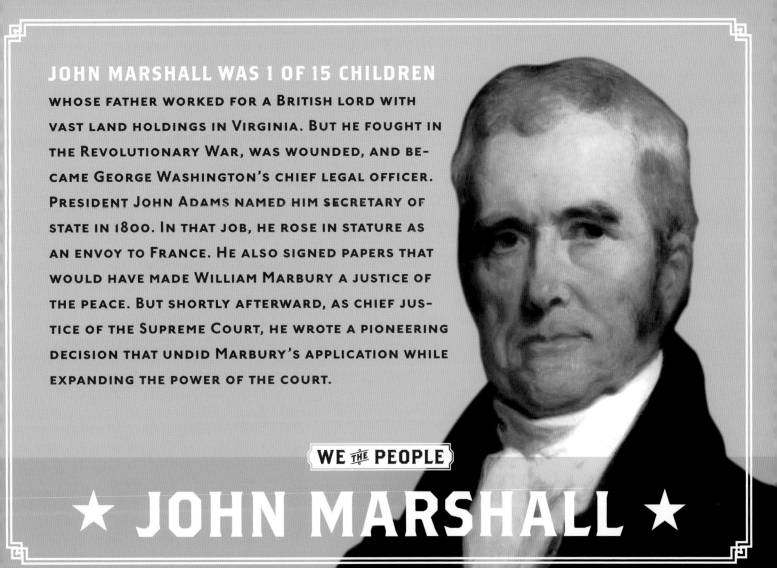

JOHN MARSHALL WAS 1 OF 15 CHILDREN WHOSE FATHER WORKED FOR A BRITISH LORD WITH VAST LAND HOLDINGS IN VIRGINIA. BUT HE FOUGHT IN THE REVOLUTIONARY WAR, WAS WOUNDED, AND BECAME GEORGE WASHINGTON'S CHIEF LEGAL OFFICER. PRESIDENT JOHN ADAMS NAMED HIM SECRETARY OF STATE IN 1800. IN THAT JOB, HE ROSE IN STATURE AS AN ENVOY TO FRANCE. HE ALSO SIGNED PAPERS THAT WOULD HAVE MADE WILLIAM MARBURY A JUSTICE OF THE PEACE. BUT SHORTLY AFTERWARD, AS CHIEF JUSTICE OF THE SUPREME COURT, HE WROTE A PIONEERING DECISION THAT UNDID MARBURY'S APPLICATION WHILE EXPANDING THE POWER OF THE COURT.

★ JOHN MARSHALL ★

service of the new country turned down judgeships. Alexander Hamilton, a key designer of the Constitution, and Patrick Henry, the former Virginia governor and Revolutionary War hero, refused to accept nominations for the job. John Jay, appointed by president George Washington as the first chief justice, called the demands "in a degree intolerable," and threatened to resign. By 1793, Congress scaled back the circuit court hearings to once a year. Jay resigned anyway in 1795 to become governor of New York, a career move that would never happen today.

When president John Adams appointed John Marshall chief justice, the Supreme Court's status rose dramatically. Marshall brought stability to the court. His 34 years is the longest of any chief justice in history. Marshall had been appointed secretary

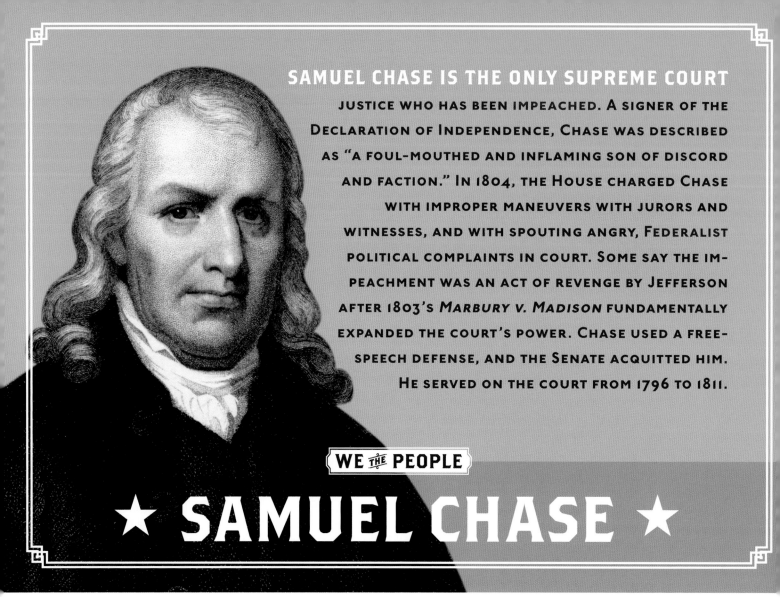

★ SAMUEL CHASE ★

SAMUEL CHASE IS THE ONLY SUPREME COURT JUSTICE WHO HAS BEEN IMPEACHED. A SIGNER OF THE DECLARATION OF INDEPENDENCE, CHASE WAS DESCRIBED AS "A FOUL-MOUTHED AND INFLAMING SON OF DISCORD AND FACTION." IN 1804, THE HOUSE CHARGED CHASE WITH IMPROPER MANEUVERS WITH JURORS AND WITNESSES, AND WITH SPOUTING ANGRY, FEDERALIST POLITICAL COMPLAINTS IN COURT. SOME SAY THE IMPEACHMENT WAS AN ACT OF REVENGE BY JEFFERSON AFTER 1803's *MARBURY V. MADISON* FUNDAMENTALLY EXPANDED THE COURT'S POWER. CHASE USED A FREE-SPEECH DEFENSE, AND THE SENATE ACQUITTED HIM. HE SERVED ON THE COURT FROM 1796 TO 1811.

of state by Adams near the end of Adams's term. He was named chief justice six months later, in 1801, and briefly held both jobs. Marshall's court soon heard William Marbury's case. Marbury's appointment to a federal position was being delayed by President Jefferson and his secretary of state, James Madison. Marbury's lawsuit became known as *Marbury v. Madison*. (Court cases are almost always titled with the names of the parties suing or accusing each other. The letter *v* in the middle stands for the Latin word "versus," meaning "against.")

In deciding *Marbury v. Madison*, Marshall and his five fellow justices determined that the Constitution didn't give the court **jurisdiction** in the case. Even though that meant backing away from making a decision on Marbury's right to the job,

the court identified a much greater principle. It established that the courts have the power to determine whether laws passed by Congress, states, or other local governments are in keeping with the Constitution. That power, known as judicial review, allows the courts to undo actions taken by the president or by legislative bodies. It is one of the most potent abilities the Supreme Court possesses. Coincidentally, Madison had argued for such a court-based power in the *Federalist Papers*. These were essays he, Jay, and Hamilton had written to promote the Constitution and a strong central government. Madison wrote that

> Thirty-nine delegates signed the U.S. Constitution at Independence Hall in 1787.

★ *Marbury v. Madison* became the first of dozens of Supreme Court opinions in which the court played a major role in the design of government—and sometimes social—policy. ★

A SLOW START

interpretation of the law was better left to appointed judges than to elected legislatures caught up in political controversies. *Marbury v. Madison* became the first of dozens of Supreme Court opinions in which the court played a major role in the design of government—and sometimes social—policy. (Supreme Court decisions are known as "opinions.")

Some of the court's rulings in the first half of the 19th century reinforced slavery. In 1857, the court under chief justice Roger Taney found that slaves, even freed ones, had no

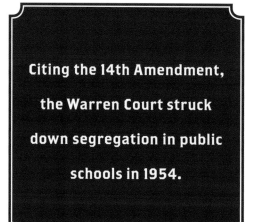

Citing the 14th Amendment, the Warren Court struck down segregation in public schools in 1954.

rights to citizenship. An 1896 opinion, *Plessy v. Ferguson*, affirmed the practice of offering blacks-only and whites-only train cars, drinking fountains, schools, and other public facilities. But 58 years later, that policy of segregation was declared unconstitutional by a unanimous Supreme Court in *Brown v. Board of Education*.

In recent decades, the Supreme Court has been pivotal in determining key features of the death penalty, **abortion**, freedom of speech and religion, freedom of the press, and civil rights. It has also delivered the final

The News

HIGH COURT BANS SEGREGATION IN PUBLIC SCHOOLS

THE 2016 SUPREME COURT JUSTICES

SAMUEL A. ALITO

STEPHEN G. BREYER

RUTH BADER GINSBURG

ELENA KAGAN

ANTHONY M. KENNEDY

CHIEF JUSTICE JOHN G. ROBERTS

ANTONIN SCALIA
until his February 2016 death

SONIA SOTOMAYOR

CLARENCE THOMAS

RONALD REAGAN

A SLOW START

word on numerous aspects of financial law. While the court often reflects the thinking of its time, it can also be slow to respond. Because its members serve lifetime appointments, they may not be in a hurry to decide a case. Since 1790, only 112 people have served on the Supreme Court.

There have been nine seats on the Supreme Court since 1869. Before then, the number fluctuated. In 1863, there were 10 positions on the bench. The first woman on the Supreme Court was Sandra Day O'Connor, nominated by president Ronald Reagan in 1981. She served until 2006. In 2016, three women were on the court: Elena Kagan, Sonia Sotomayor, and Ruth Bader Ginsburg.

> Though four women had served on the Supreme Court by 2016, none had been appointed chief justice.

THE MARSHALL COURT
1801–35

THE WARREN COURT
1953–69

THE JAY, RUTLEDGE, AND ELLSWORTH COURTS
1789–1800

THE REHNQUIST COURT
1986–2005

THE ROBERTS COURT
2005–present

THE TANEY COURT
1836–64

SUPREME COURT ERAS

THE HUGHES, STONE, AND VINSON COURTS
1930–53

THE CHASE, WAITE, AND FULLER COURTS
1864–1910

THE BURGER COURT
1969–86

THE WHITE AND TAFT COURTS
1910–30

CHAPTER 2

EACH COURT MAKES A MARK

THE U.S. SUPREME COURT

When a president nominates someone to fill a spot on the Supreme Court, one of the most vivid examples of the balance of power is revealed. The president's nominee must be approved by a majority vote of 51 in the U.S. Senate. This gives at least part of the legislative branch an opportunity to make a statement about a presidential action while deciding who will fill a key position in the judicial branch.

The Senate vote follows what may be lengthy confirmation hearings. Sometimes these hearings generate intense public interest. A 2005 essay by the Center for American Progress, listing the wide-ranging controversies the Supreme Court may be expected to deal with, argued that the Senate should carefully examine a nominee's **ideology**. "The judges who decide these questions should have the character, training, life experience,

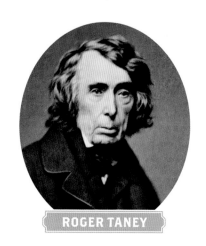

★ [The Taney] court's decision in *Dred Scott v. Sandford* (1857) overturned a congressional act passed in 1820 that had been intended to preserve the Union. ★

EACH COURT MAKES A MARK

and breadth of understanding to appreciate the meaning and significance of the cases that come before them," the essay stated.

Indeed, congressional nomination hearings often air out some of the most heated feelings of the day. Senators may use the hearings to attack a president for a policy or order he has authorized. Sometimes they veer off in unexpected directions. When Clarence Thomas was nominated in 1991, a law professor and former colleague accused him of sexual harassment. The hearings then became a major media event, focusing more on male-female relationships in the workplace. Thomas called it "a high-tech **lynching**." Nevertheless, Thomas was approved

by a 52–48 vote.

A rejected nomination can be an embarrassment for a president. Only two presidents, Richard Nixon and Grover Cleveland, had two nominees rejected. But Nixon had four confirmed and Cleveland had two.

Supreme Court eras are named for each chief justice. The Marshall Court (1801–35) made a lasting mark by establishing the power of judicial review. But it also gave Congress the right to set up banks and regulate interstate commerce.

Marshall's successor, Roger Taney, presided for the next 28 years. His court's decision in *Dred Scott v. Sandford* (1857) overturned a congressional act passed in 1820 that had been intended to preserve the Union. But

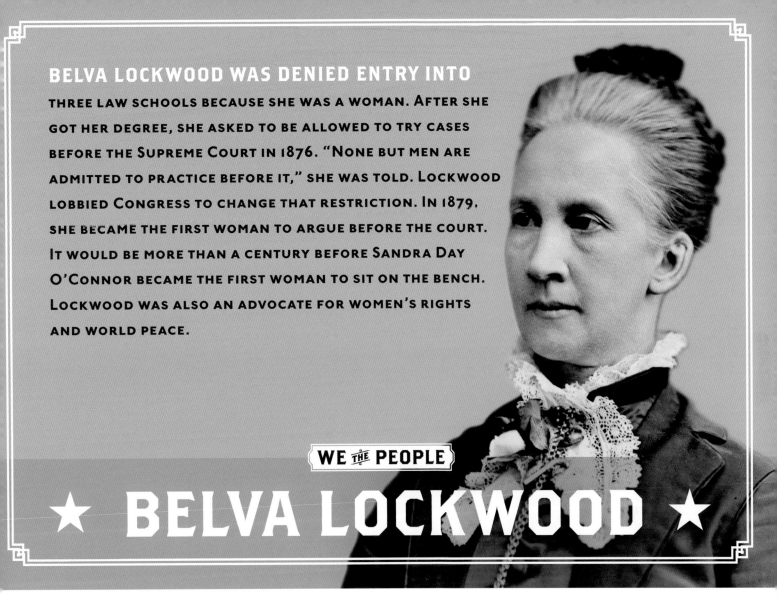

BELVA LOCKWOOD WAS DENIED ENTRY INTO THREE LAW SCHOOLS BECAUSE SHE WAS A WOMAN. AFTER SHE GOT HER DEGREE, SHE ASKED TO BE ALLOWED TO TRY CASES BEFORE THE SUPREME COURT IN 1876. "NONE BUT MEN ARE ADMITTED TO PRACTICE BEFORE IT," SHE WAS TOLD. LOCKWOOD LOBBIED CONGRESS TO CHANGE THAT RESTRICTION. IN 1879, SHE BECAME THE FIRST WOMAN TO ARGUE BEFORE THE COURT. IT WOULD BE MORE THAN A CENTURY BEFORE SANDRA DAY O'CONNOR BECAME THE FIRST WOMAN TO SIT ON THE BENCH. LOCKWOOD WAS ALSO AN ADVOCATE FOR WOMEN'S RIGHTS AND WORLD PEACE.

WE THE PEOPLE

★ BELVA LOCKWOOD ★

the Civil War raged during the final years of Taney's term. In 1865, just one year after his death, the states took the issue of slavery out of the court's hands. They approved the 13th Amendment to the Constitution, abolishing the practice.

Chief justice Salmon P. Chase (1864–73) directed the Senate's impeachment trial of president Andrew Johnson. Johnson survived by one vote. Chase's term also saw two amendments to the Constitution. One, the 14th Amendment, tossed the *Dred Scott* opinion onto the legal trash heap by extending citizenship to slaves. Its clause guaranteeing "equal protection" under the law to all people is one of the most frequently cited provisions in federal court cases.

The Melville Fuller Court (1888–1910) began to break up **monopolies**, including Standard Oil. It also decided several cases

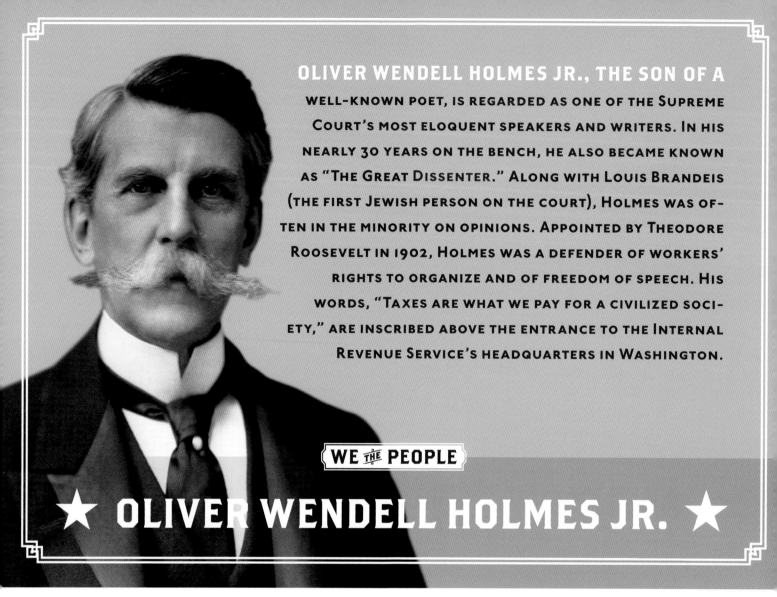

OLIVER WENDELL HOLMES JR., THE SON OF A WELL-KNOWN POET, IS REGARDED AS ONE OF THE SUPREME COURT'S MOST ELOQUENT SPEAKERS AND WRITERS. IN HIS NEARLY 30 YEARS ON THE BENCH, HE ALSO BECAME KNOWN AS "THE GREAT DISSENTER." ALONG WITH LOUIS BRANDEIS (THE FIRST JEWISH PERSON ON THE COURT), HOLMES WAS OFTEN IN THE MINORITY ON OPINIONS. APPOINTED BY THEODORE ROOSEVELT IN 1902, HOLMES WAS A DEFENDER OF WORKERS' RIGHTS TO ORGANIZE AND OF FREEDOM OF SPEECH. HIS WORDS, "TAXES ARE WHAT WE PAY FOR A CIVILIZED SOCIETY," ARE INSCRIBED ABOVE THE ENTRANCE TO THE INTERNAL REVENUE SERVICE'S HEADQUARTERS IN WASHINGTON.

WE THE PEOPLE

★ OLIVER WENDELL HOLMES JR. ★

over workday length and workplace safety in favor of the workers. But in 1896, the Fuller Court established the idea that racially "separate but equal" facilities such as trains and schools were acceptable. This decision made racial segregation possible for the next 58 years. In many places in the U.S., people were denied equal treatment because of the color of their skin.

Former U.S. president William Howard

Taft became chief justice in 1921, the only person to achieve both the presidency and the leadership of the Supreme Court. Taft streamlined the Supreme Court's work, essentially getting Congress to let the court decide whether to hear a case or not. In the view of former justice Sandra Day O'Connor, Taft's term "marked the birth of the modern Supreme Court."

The Charles Evans Hughes Court

(1930–41) nearly sparked a Constitutional crisis. It struck down two key features of president Franklin D. Roosevelt's **New Deal** laws, calling them unconstitutional. This frustrated Roosevelt. He commented that the justices were old and overworked, and he proposed naming as many as six additional judges to the nine-person bench. That may have shocked the court into changing course. Enthusiasm for altering the makeup of the court soon faded. It even began to be seen as a potentially dangerous tampering with the balance of power outlined in the Constitution. Congress turned its attention to passing more laws that expanded the role of

> The New Deal programs were intended to bring the U.S. out of the Great Depression.

★ The Warren Burger Court (1969–86) ... influenced a broad sweep of issues during a tumultuous time in American society. ★

EACH COURT MAKES A MARK

the federal government. These included the 1935 Social Security Act.

In one of its first orders of business, the Earl Warren Court (1953–69) declared in 1954 that the "separate but equal" idea "has no place" in public education. This reversed the Fuller Court's ruling of 1896. The Warren Court also declared that every defendant, even the poorest, has a right to representation in court by an attorney. In 1966, *Miranda v. Arizona* set down the now-famous concept of *Miranda* rights. Namely, this made sure that any arrested person must be told, "You have the right to remain silent."

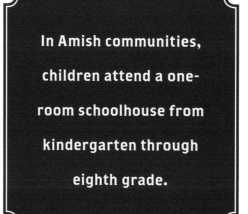

In Amish communities, children attend a one-room schoolhouse from kindergarten through eighth grade.

The Warren Burger Court (1969–86) likewise influenced a broad sweep of issues during a tumultuous time in American society. It agreed that Amish children should not be forced to attend public school if it's against their religion. Then it reaffirmed that the government cannot prevent publication of secret government documents. The Burger Court also dealt with issues regarding the First Amendment's guarantee of freedom of speech. In 1974, the court ruled that President Nixon did not have an "executive privilege" to

COURT HOME

Prior to the 1935 opening of the Supreme Court Building, the court met in various locations in New York City, Philadelphia, and Washington, D.C. From 1860 to 1935, the court met in the Old Senate Chamber in the U.S. Capitol.

SENIORITY

The chief justice begins each conference discussion with a summary, then the justices speak in order of seniority. The justices are also seated by seniority. If two justices are sworn in on the same day, seniority is determined by age.

ON CURRENCY

JOHN MARSHALL and **SALMON P. CHASE** are the only justices to appear on U.S. currency. Marshall was featured on the $500 bill, while Chase was on the $10,000 bill. The bills were discontinued in 1969 and are no longer in circulation.

32

YOUNGEST

The youngest appointed justice, **JOSEPH STORY**, was sworn in at the age of 32. He served from 1811 to 1845.

65

OLDEST

The oldest appointed justice, **HORACE H. LURTON**, was sworn in at the age of 65. He served from 1910 to 1914.

HILLARY CLINTON

withhold tapes of secret conversations from prosecutors, effectively pushing him toward resignation. The year before, the court had carved out a right still being bitterly opposed today—a woman's right to an abortion.

The William H. Rehnquist Court (1986–2005) ventured into questions raised by new technologies, such as privacy in the face of electronic surveillance and the right to die. Rehnquist himself presided over the impeachment trial of president Bill Clinton. But his court's most visible and controversial ruling may have been to stop a vote recount in Florida. This threw the 2000 presidential election to George W. Bush, after former vice president Al Gore had won the popular vote.

As of 2016, one of the John G. Roberts Court's most far-reaching opinions involved campaign financing. *Citizens United v. FEC* stemmed from a political group's efforts to broadcast a film critical of presidential candidate Hillary Clinton in 2008. The court struck down an earlier law and allowed corporations and labor unions to make unlimited contributions toward political messages (such as films and advertisements) independent of candidates' campaigns. The decision was widely criticized for allowing too much money into campaigns, particularly from already-wealthy interest groups.

Outside campaign spending has more than doubled since the court's 2010 *Citizens United v. FEC* opinion.

THE ROAD 🏛️ THE SUPREME COURT

U.S. DISTRICT COURTS

LOCAL 2ND STATE TRIAL COURTS

ORIGINAL JURISDICTION

U.S. COURTS OF APPEALS

STATE SUPREME COURTS

UNITED STATES SUPREME COURT

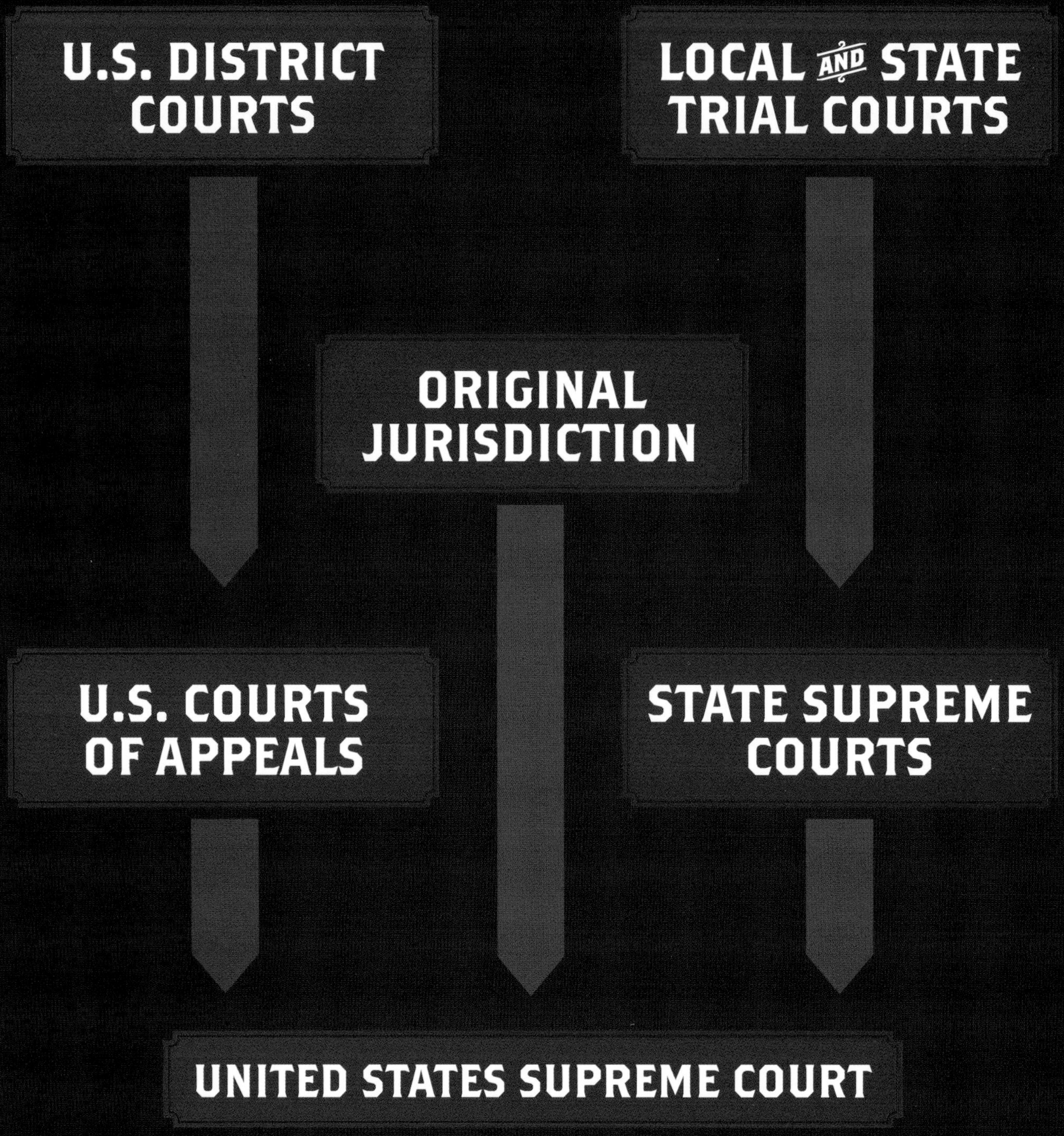

☛ Of the three paths a case may take on its way to the U.S. Supreme Court, the most common is via the federal circuit, or the Courts of Appeals.

CHAPTER 3

THE ROAD TO THE SUPREME COURT

THE U.S. SUPREME COURT

Sometimes your chore list at home or your math grade at school seems so unfair you might want to take it to the Supreme Court. But you're probably going to have to find another way to settle the dispute. U.S. federal and state courts hear about 27 million cases per year. Of those, only about 100 are accepted for a hearing by the Supreme Court.

The Supreme Court is rarely the court where cases are heard first. The ones that are, according to the Constitution, are those involving treaties, foreign officials, and arguments between states. In such cases, the court has what's called "original jurisdiction." The rest of the court's caseload is "appellate," involving decisions made in lower courts that have been appealed. Originally, the court was required to review all appeals from lower federal courts. That became too much work, though. It also

★ There are 94 U.S. district courts in the federal system. ★

THE ROAD TO THE SUPREME COURT

delayed decisions for years. The 1891 creation of the U.S. Court of Appeals and later reforms helped. Now the court chooses its cases. Much of its work involves reviewing the work of other courts and sometimes correcting it. But that's as far as a case can go. Only a Constitutional amendment can reverse a Supreme Court ruling.

From divorces to criminal acts, most cases are handled in the hundreds of local and state courts in the U.S. When decisions in those cases are questioned, they follow each state's appeal process. This usually ends at a state supreme court. State supreme court cases can be appealed into the federal court system. It's still a long way from there to the U.S. Supreme Court, though.

There are 94 U.S. district courts in the federal system. There is at least one in each state as well as in the District of Columbia, Puerto Rico, and the three U.S. territories. District courts are where trials are held in both criminal and **civil** cases. Any case involving residents of different states starts in a federal rather than state court. Cases of criminal activity that crossed state borders, such as kidnapping or drug dealing, often begin in federal district court, too. The 94 district courts are organized into 12 federal circuits. Each of these has a U.S. Court of Appeals to handle disputes over decisions by district courts. The next and last stop is the U.S. Supreme Court.

The first thing the Supreme Court does

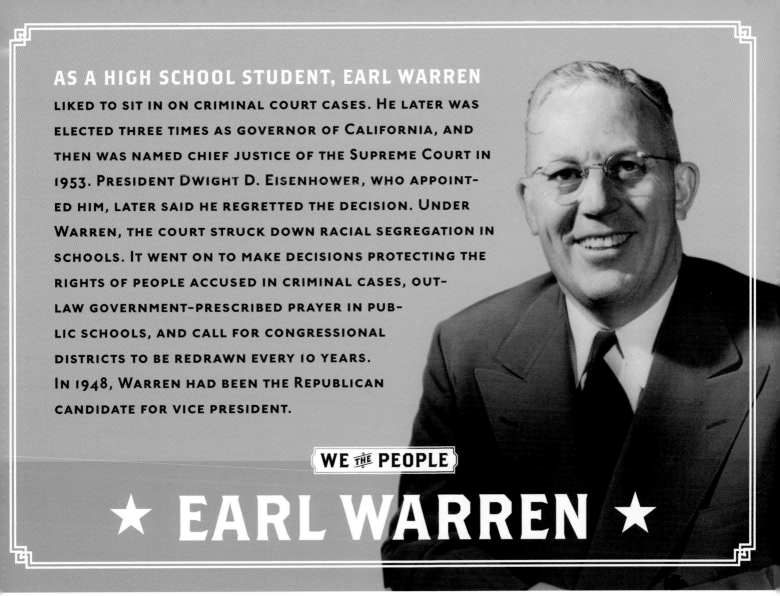

AS A HIGH SCHOOL STUDENT, EARL WARREN LIKED TO SIT IN ON CRIMINAL COURT CASES. HE LATER WAS ELECTED THREE TIMES AS GOVERNOR OF CALIFORNIA, AND THEN WAS NAMED CHIEF JUSTICE OF THE SUPREME COURT IN 1953. PRESIDENT DWIGHT D. EISENHOWER, WHO APPOINTED HIM, LATER SAID HE REGRETTED THE DECISION. UNDER WARREN, THE COURT STRUCK DOWN RACIAL SEGREGATION IN SCHOOLS. IT WENT ON TO MAKE DECISIONS PROTECTING THE RIGHTS OF PEOPLE ACCUSED IN CRIMINAL CASES, OUTLAW GOVERNMENT-PRESCRIBED PRAYER IN PUBLIC SCHOOLS, AND CALL FOR CONGRESSIONAL DISTRICTS TO BE REDRAWN EVERY 10 YEARS. IN 1948, WARREN HAD BEEN THE REPUBLICAN CANDIDATE FOR VICE PRESIDENT.

WE THE PEOPLE

★ EARL WARREN ★

after agreeing to hear a case is ask the lower court for its records. This is called issuing a "writ of certiorari." *Certiorari* comes from a Latin word meaning "inform." The Supreme Court gets about 8,000 petitions for writs of certiorari each year. It grants approximately 100 of those.

Then attorneys for each side must submit their arguments in documents no longer than 50 pages. That might sound long,

but they're known as "briefs." Briefs summarize the case and offer reasons why the court should decide in favor of one side and not the other. They almost always describe how earlier Supreme Courts or other federal courts have decided similar cases. Such decisions are known as "precedents." They are the building blocks of the U.S. judicial system.

Other parties interested in the case

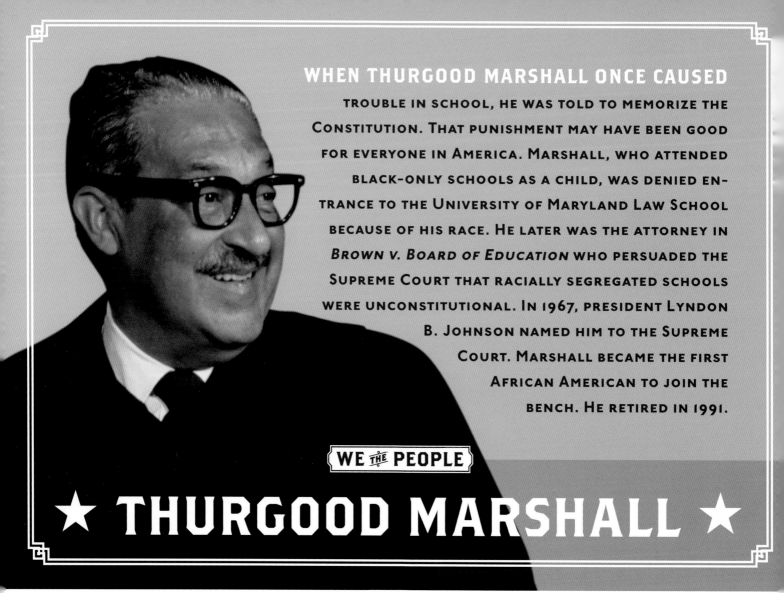

WHEN THURGOOD MARSHALL ONCE CAUSED TROUBLE IN SCHOOL, HE WAS TOLD TO MEMORIZE THE CONSTITUTION. THAT PUNISHMENT MAY HAVE BEEN GOOD FOR EVERYONE IN AMERICA. MARSHALL, WHO ATTENDED BLACK-ONLY SCHOOLS AS A CHILD, WAS DENIED ENTRANCE TO THE UNIVERSITY OF MARYLAND LAW SCHOOL BECAUSE OF HIS RACE. HE LATER WAS THE ATTORNEY IN *BROWN V. BOARD OF EDUCATION* WHO PERSUADED THE SUPREME COURT THAT RACIALLY SEGREGATED SCHOOLS WERE UNCONSTITUTIONAL. IN 1967, PRESIDENT LYNDON B. JOHNSON NAMED HIM TO THE SUPREME COURT. MARSHALL BECAME THE FIRST AFRICAN AMERICAN TO JOIN THE BENCH. HE RETIRED IN 1991.

WE THE PEOPLE

★ THURGOOD MARSHALL ★

might submit their own briefs seeking a certain outcome. Each of those parties is known as "amicus curiae," another Latin term meaning "friend of the court." Their briefs must be no more than 30 pages.

After briefs come oral arguments. This is where attorneys for each side speak to the court and take questions from the justices. The attorneys have just 30 minutes to present a case that may have already been

through dozens of trials and hearings. One notable exception to the timetable came in 1974's **Watergate scandal** case. Attorneys for president Richard Nixon had three hours to try to persuade the court that Nixon had an "executive privilege" to withhold tape-recorded conversations from prosecutors. In what was a critical moment for the government's balance of power, the court disagreed. The president was forced

to hand over the tapes.

The only deadline for a written opinion from the court is the end of that court's annual session. (The Supreme Court's year runs from the first Monday in October to early June.) If the court can't reach a resolution that year, the case must be reheard, with new briefs,

in the next session.

A lot happens between each of the steps. The justices meet weekly and discuss the petitions for writs of certiorari. The court hears oral arguments in four cases (one hour each) on Mondays, Tuesdays, and Thursdays. Then the justices and their **law clerks** set about doing

> Nixon stepped down to avoid his inevitable impeachment.

> ★ A court's opinions are written and signed by justices. If the chief justice is in the majority, he or she writes the opinion ... Justices who disagree with the majority might write a dissenting opinion. Such opinions may be strongly worded. ★

further research and perhaps beginning to write an opinion.

In continuing conferences, justices talk over their thoughts about a case. They may exchange drafts of decisions. Most cases are decided when five of the court's nine justices (a majority) agree. The court's findings are final.

A court's opinions are written and signed by justices. If the chief justice is in the majority, he or she writes the opinion or assigns a justice to write it. If not, that task goes to the longest-serving justice in the majority. Justices who disagree with the majority might write a dissenting opinion. Such opinions may be strongly worded. After the Japanese bombed the American naval base at Pearl Harbor in 1941, the court upheld an army order. It called for the removal of Japanese American residents from their homes along the West Coast and placed them in holding camps. Justice Frank Murphy, one of three dissenters, called it "a clear violation of Constitutional rights" and "utterly revolting among a free people."

Sometimes a justice will agree with the majority's decision but for far different

Congress declared war against Japan on December 8th, 1941, the day after the attack on Pearl Harbor.

BROWN V. BOARD OF EDUCATION

ON MAY 17, 1954, THE SUPREME COURT ANNOUNCED ITS UNANIMOUS DECISION TO END SEGREGATION IN PUBLIC SCHOOLS.

In the early 1950s more than a third of states segregated public schools by law. Black schools received less funding than white schools, and many lacked proper facilities and resources. In 1951, Oliver Brown and several other African American parents sued the Topeka, Kansas school district for violating the 14th Amendment. The case reached the Supreme Court, where it was merged with four other school-segregation cases, in 1953. The court found "separate educational facilities ... inherently unequal" and, overruling *Plessy v. Ferguson*, declared segregation unconstitutional.

THE COURT RULED THAT SEGREGATED SCHOOLS VIOLATED THE 14TH AMENDMENT.

☞ National guardsmen protected students in areas where schools were reluctant to integrate.

AL GORE

reasons. He or she may then write a concurring opinion. Justices sometimes sign more than one dissenting or concurring opinion. And when there is no majority, more justices may line up behind one opinion than the others. That outcome might see four justices with one opinion, three with another, and two with a third.

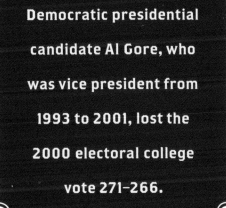

Democratic presidential candidate Al Gore, who was vice president from 1993 to 2001, lost the 2000 electoral college vote 271–266.

One famously unanimous opinion was for *Brown v. Board of Education.* It was written by chief justice Earl Warren without any concurring opinions. It was important to Warren that the entire court agree on that opinion. He didn't want to suggest there was any room for further practice of racial segregation in the South. Far less convincing was the decision in *Bush v. Gore,* the case that resolved the 2000 presidential election. That outcome was 5–4.

INTERPRETS **AND** CLARIFIES THE CONSTITUTION

EXERCISES JUDICIAL REVIEW **AND** OVERRULES LAWS IT FINDS TO BE UNCONSTITUTIONAL

ENSURES THAT EACH BRANCH **OF** GOVERNMENT DOES NOT ATTEMPT TO TRANSCEND ITS CONSTITUTIONAL POWERS

THE HIGHEST COURT IN THE U.S. **AND** THE FINAL PLACE WHERE CASES CAN BE APPEALED

CHAPTER 4

CONSTRUCTION AHEAD

THE U.S. SUPREME COURT

On paper, the Supreme Court's duties seem simple enough. It examines presidential orders, acts of Congress or other legislatures, and court decisions to decide whether they're Constitutional. If the court decides some measure is unconstitutional, there are three possible responses: change the law, change its enforcement, or change the Constitution.

The first option, changing the law, is the easiest and most frequent response. The second, changing the enforcement practice, is often more difficult. After the court ruled in *Miranda v. Arizona* that arrested suspects must be reminded of their rights, police departments across the country printed wallet cards for their officers to reference. *Brown v. Board of Education* called for all schools to be racially desegregated, but it didn't say how that should be done. Some districts simply allowed kids to go to

★ **"Loose" or "broad constructionists" believe the Constitution provides rights and powers not only through what the framers wrote but also through what they implied. Thomas Jefferson was an early critic of loose construction.** ★

CONSTRUCTION AHEAD

the schools nearest their homes in mixed neighborhoods. Many put kids on buses to schools much farther away to achieve a racial mix. Others closed schools entirely. Decades later, **magnet schools** emerged.

The third option, passing a Constitutional amendment, is much more difficult and rare. First, it requires that a bill pass both houses of Congress, then be approved by three-fourths of state legislatures. (Seven of the 27 amendments to the Constitution were intended to negate Supreme Court decisions.) The most vivid example of the difficulties in passing an amendment is the 27th Amendment. That measure, about the timing of congressional pay raises, was passed by Congress in 1789 but not approved by the

states until 1992. That was a 203-year effort!

Hard though it may be to overcome unpopular decisions by the Supreme Court, that's not what drives most recent criticisms of the court. Since the beginning, there has been a tension between two ways of putting the Constitution to work. "Strict constructionists" are judges who believe the Constitution means exactly what it says. "Loose" or "broad constructionists" believe the Constitution provides rights and powers not only through what the framers wrote but also through what they implied. Thomas Jefferson was an early critic of loose construction. In 1803, he warned that chief justice John Marshall's establishment of judicial review—not mentioned in the

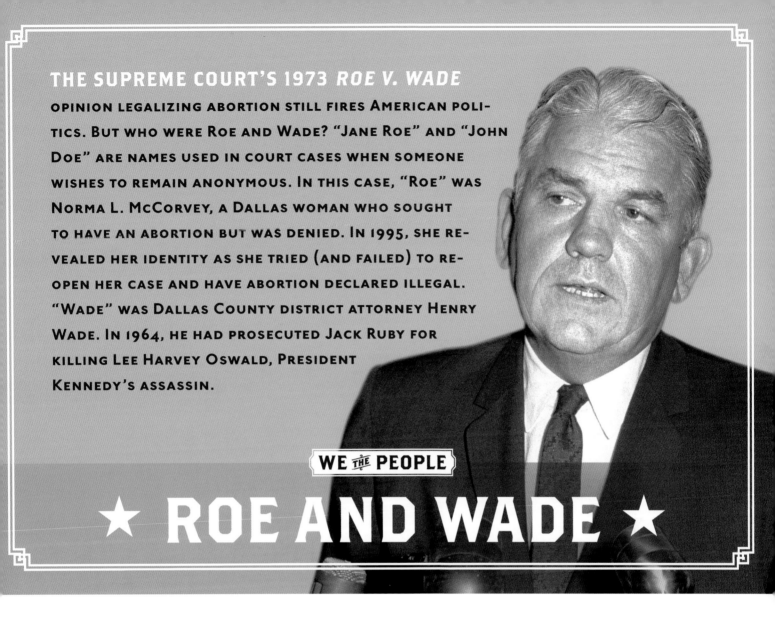

THE SUPREME COURT'S 1973 *ROE V. WADE* OPINION LEGALIZING ABORTION STILL FIRES AMERICAN POLITICS. BUT WHO WERE ROE AND WADE? "JANE ROE" AND "JOHN DOE" ARE NAMES USED IN COURT CASES WHEN SOMEONE WISHES TO REMAIN ANONYMOUS. IN THIS CASE, "ROE" WAS NORMA L. McCORVEY, A DALLAS WOMAN WHO SOUGHT TO HAVE AN ABORTION BUT WAS DENIED. IN 1995, SHE REVEALED HER IDENTITY AS SHE TRIED (AND FAILED) TO REOPEN HER CASE AND HAVE ABORTION DECLARED ILLEGAL. "WADE" WAS DALLAS COUNTY DISTRICT ATTORNEY HENRY WADE. IN 1964, HE HAD PROSECUTED JACK RUBY FOR KILLING LEE HARVEY OSWALD, PRESIDENT KENNEDY'S ASSASSIN.

WE THE PEOPLE

★ ROE AND WADE ★

Constitution—had put the Supreme Court on the road to absolute power.

Especially since the Warren Court of the 1950s and '60s, critics have charged the court with engaging in a form of loose constructionism known as judicial activism. Basically, that's a term that describes how courts can deliver rulings that offer new interpretations of the Constitution. Both **liberals** and **conservatives** have alternately described it as an aggressive power-grab by the Supreme Court. The practice is particularly troubling, some say, because Supreme Court justices aren't elected, and their decisions are difficult to change.

Robert P. George, a law professor at both Princeton and Harvard universities, describes judicial activism from a conservative point of view. He says it is a way in which judges interpret the law to favor their

★ SONIA SOTOMAYOR ★

SONIA SOTOMAYOR GREW UP IN A HOUSING PROJECT IN NEW YORK CITY WITH PARENTS WHO SPOKE MOSTLY SPANISH. AT PRINCETON UNIVERSITY, SHE EARNED THE SCHOOL'S HIGHEST ACADEMIC HONOR. WHILE SERVING ON A U.S. DISTRICT COURT IN NEW YORK, SHE ENDED A MAJOR LEAGUE BASEBALL STRIKE IN 1995 WITH A RULING IN THE PLAYERS' FAVOR. IN 2009, SHE BECAME THE FIRST HISPANIC SUPREME COURT JUSTICE. IN 2015, SHE WAS IN THE MAJORITY ON DECISIONS LEGALIZING SAME-SEX MARRIAGE IN ALL STATES AND UPHOLDING A KEY PROVISION OF THE AFFORDABLE CARE ACT. HER 2013 AUTOBIOGRAPHY, "MY BELOVED WORLD," WAS A *NEW YORK TIMES* BESTSELLER.

personal beliefs rather than the Constitution, particularly when it comes to social issues. It involves finding rights in the Constitution that aren't stated in writing. According to George, it first emerged in the *Dred Scott* opinion of 1857. In that case, George says, the Taney Court appeared to be protecting the minority rights of slaveholders, but it also reinforced the broader institution of slavery. A 1905 case, *Lochner v. New York*, saw a law

limiting bakery workers' weeks to 60 hours declared by the Fuller Court to be unconstitutional. It infringed on an unwritten law on contracts, the court said. The decision was rolled back by the Hughes Court in 1937, but George notes that it was well in keeping with the pro-business leanings of the earlier Fuller Court.

Judicial activism might have had its fiercest practitioner, George writes, in justice

William O. Douglas. He served 36 years on the court, the longest term of any justice. In a 1965 majority opinion that struck down a Connecticut law against birth control, Douglas cited a "right to **marital** privacy" that is not stated in the Constitution. (A previous justice, Louis Brandeis, discussed the right to privacy in an essay in 1890, but many people have questioned its legal roots.) The right to privacy then became a key factor in the 1973 *Roe v. Wade* opinion that struck down bans on abortion. As an avid outdoorsman, Douglas also became a champion of environmental causes. He wrote opinions urging that natural features such as trees

> An 1873 law criminalized the advertisement and distribution of contraceptives.

★ Civil rights, labor law, voting rights, criminal justice procedure, gun rights, and business regulation will no doubt remain regular features on the court's docket. So will controversial issues such as immigration and universal healthcare. ★

and rivers should have legal rights.

Another conservative author, Clint Bolick, vice president of the Goldwater Institute in Phoenix, Arizona, argues that some judicial activism may be necessary. It's a way of protecting the court's Constitutional powers. Courts should not, for example, deliver decisions that raise taxes or interfere with school systems, Bolick writes. Those are not powers granted by the Constitution. But courts should keep asserting their powers to limit excesses of the other branches of government. "Courts that merely rubber-stamp legislation or executive branch decisions ... evade their essential Constitutional role," Bolick writes.

Familiar issues are likely to continue arriving on the Supreme Court's doorstep. Civil rights, labor law, voting rights, criminal justice procedure, gun rights, and business regulation will no doubt remain regular features on the court's **docket**. So will controversial issues such as immigration and universal healthcare. Nominees to the Supreme Court are certain to find themselves being questioned intensely on their position on the

> As ships made their way to the federal immigration station on Ellis Island, the Statue of Liberty became a symbol of freedom and opportunity.

PRIVACY RIGHTS WILL LIKELY BE AT THE CENTER OF DISPUTES OVER COMMUNICATION AND SUR- VEILLANCE TECHNOLOGIES.

WHAT ARE LEGAL AND ILLEGAL USES OF SOCIAL MEDIA AND THE INTERNET?

CAN THE GOVERNMENT WATCH WHAT CITIZENS DO?

HOW WILL UNMANNED AIRCRAFT BE USED?

JAMES MADISON

constitutionality of *Roe v. Wade*, as they have been for more than four decades.

But the rapid pace of technological and social change in the U.S. is also likely to bring new issues to the Supreme Court. The still-fuzzy right to privacy will likely be at the center of disputes over the use of communications and surveillance technology. How far can the government go in watching what citizens do? What's legal and illegal in how all of us use social media and the Internet in general? How much people-watching by unmanned aircraft will be allowed? There is a fine line between guarding against terrorism and unfairly targeting people for surveillance, and the Supreme Court will likely be asked to draw a bolder one.

The authors of the Constitution probably never dreamed of instant global communication or drones. They clearly had a hard time envisioning black people who weren't slaves. But times change, and the Supreme Court has changed with them, often slowly, and sometimes requiring do-overs. As new crises and controversies emerge, the Supreme Court will continue to have the final word on the rules the nation lives by.

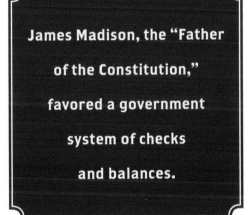

James Madison, the "Father of the Constitution," favored a government system of checks and balances.

abortion termination of a pregnancy by surgical or other medical means

civil in law, describing a legal conflict (not involving a crime) between two or more parties

conservatives in American politics, those who support social values set by tradition and favor a smaller governmental presence in everyday life and business

dissenter a person who publicly expresses disagreement

docket in court, a list or schedule of cases to be heard

Federalist an early American political party that favored a strong central government

ideology a body of ideas that guide the actions of a person or political movement

impeached brought formal charges against a government official for crimes committed while in office

jurisdiction the right, power, or authority to administer justice

law clerks in the Supreme Court, law school graduates who help a judge with research and analysis of a case, and often help write his or her decision

liberals in American politics, those who support social justice issues and favor progressive governmental involvement in public issues such as healthcare and education

lynching the execution of a person, usually by hanging, by an unauthorized mob

magnet schools public schools that emphasize particular subject offerings as a way of attracting students from broader areas and achieving a racial mix

marital having to do with marriage

maritime having to do with the sea

monopolies exclusive control of commodities or services in particular markets, often allowing the control of prices

New Deal a series of initiatives intended to ease the effects of the Great Depression, including banking reform, employment programs, and Social Security

Watergate scandal the events that led to the resignation of president Richard M. Nixon; it began with a burglary at the Watergate Hotel in Washington, D.C.

SELECTED BIBLIOGRAPHY

Baum, Lawrence. *The Supreme Court*. 8th ed. Washington, D.C.: CQ Press, 2004.

Benoit, Peter. *The Supreme Court*. New York: Children's Press, 2014.

Epstein, Lita. *The Complete Idiot's Guide to the Supreme Court*. Indianapolis, Ind.: Alpha Books, 2004.

Haerens, Margaret, ed. *The U.S. Supreme Court*. Farmington Hills, Mich.: Greenhaven Press, 2010.

O'Connor, Sandra Day. *Out of Order: Stories from the History of the Supreme Court*. New York: Random House, 2013.

Patrick, John J. *The Supreme Court of the United States: A Student Companion*. 2nd ed. New York: Oxford University Press, 2001.

WEBSITES

Congress for Kids: The Judicial Branch

www.congressforkids.net/Judicialbranch_supremecourt.htm

Review what you know about the Supreme Court with some activities.

The Supreme Court Historical Society: History of the Court

supremecourthistory.org/history_courthistory.html

Learn more about the history of each court and the lives of the justices.

Note: Every effort has been made to ensure that the websites listed above are suitable for children, that they have educational value, and that they contain no inappropriate material. However, because of the nature of the Internet, it is impossible to guarantee that these sites will remain active indefinitely or that their contents will not be altered.

Published by **Creative Education** and **Creative Paperbacks** P.O. Box 227, Mankato, Minnesota 56002 Creative Education and Creative Paperbacks are imprints of **The Creative Company** www.thecreativecompany.us

Design and production by **Christine Vanderbeek** Art direction by **Rita Marshall** Printed in China

Photographs by Alamy (ZUMA Press, Inc.), Corbis (Bettmann, Kevan Brooks/AdMedia, CORBIS, Stapleton Collection), Creative Commons Wikimedia (Brady-Handy Photograph Collection/ Library of Congress, Collection of the Supreme Court of the United States/U.S. Federal Government,

Stacey Ilys/WhiteHouse.gov, Henry Inman/Virginia Memory, Library of Congress, The Oyez Project/ Collection of the Supreme Court of the United States/U.S. Federal Government, Rembrandt Peale/The White House Historical Association, Steve Petteway/Collection of the Supreme Court of the United States/U.S. Federal Government, U.S. Capitol/U.S. Federal Government, U.S. Department of State/U.S. Federal Government, U.S. Federal Government, John Vanderlyn/The White House Historical Association), Getty Images (Fotosearch), iStockphoto (dolphinphoto, russaquarius), Shutterstock (Rob Crandall, elenabsl, Everett Historical, Evan Fariston, lkeskinen, trekandshoot)

Library of Congress Cataloging-in-Publication Data McAuliffe, Bill. The U.S. Supreme Court / Bill McAuliffe. p. cm. — (By the people) Includes bibliographical references and index. *Summary*: A historical survey of the United States Supreme Court, from its beginnings to present decisions, including its judicial role and influential justices such as Earl Warren.

ISBN 978-1-60818-678-5 *(hardcover)* **ISBN 978-1-62832-274-3** *(pbk)* **ISBN 978-1-56660-714-8** *(eBook)*

1. United States. Supreme Court—History.

KF8742.M294 2016 347.73/26—dc23   2015039279

CCSS: RI.5.1, 2, 3, 8; RI. 6.1, 2, 4, 7; RH.6-8.3, 4, 5, 6, 7, 8

First Edition HC 9 8 7 6 5 4 3 2 1 **First Edition PBK** 9 8 7 6 5 4 3 2 1

Pictured on cover: Oliver Wendell Holmes